Innovators redefine the world,

visionaries describe it,

craftsmen build it,

and God establishes it.

My Eyes See

My Eyes See

Volume 1

Joel Sejour

iUniverse, Inc.

New York Bloomington Shanghai

My Eyes See
Volume 1

iUniverse books may be ordered through booksellers or by contacting:

iUniverse
1663 Liberty Drive
Bloomington, IN 47403
www.iuniverse.com
1-800-Authors (1-800-288-4677)

Because of the dynamic nature of the Internet, any Web addresses
or links contained in this book may have changed
since publication and may no longer be valid.

The views expressed in this work are solely those of the author and do not necessarily reflect the views
of the publisher, and the publisher hereby disclaims any responsibility for them.

ISBN: 978-0-595-34807-7 (pbk)
ISBN: 978-0-595-79539-0 (ebk)

Printed in the United States of America

For Josue Sejour

My brother, my comrade

Contents

Be advised that, pertaining to the configuration of this literature, the poet chooses to express himself in a unique way. The poet knowingly and willingly writes this way, declaring its uniqueness to be his signature and fingerprint.

Introduction (The Forbidden Fruit)

This epistle is a record of every moment that I've shared with her. And she is precisely imprinted in my memory, for it is the memories alone that sustain me through the trying times. I wish I could endear her with my phrases. God endowed me with poetic grace, and still I never told her how much she meant to me.

I never spoke of love, even though I felt it. For many years of restraint, I behaved in a sophomoric fashion; I thought it was unmanly to speak about love. Luckily for me, her understanding transcended my muteness. She knew I loved her, but I never cast all her doubts asunder.

My mind will never forget her face. She is a gem more precious than any stone on earth. She was my lover and my friend. Her hair is long, black, and curly; her eyes are brown; and the complexion of her skin is caramel.

I remember the day she introduced herself to me. We shook hands. She told me her name, and I told her mine. I remember the first sentence she uttered to me: "God is love." I wish she were here with me today to see how my soul giggles when I think about her.

When we met, I was convinced we had met before, and when I began to search for answers, I remembered how I knew her. I know you've heard this proverb before: there is nothing new under the sun; what is old is new, and what's new is old.

She told me I completed her. When she was a child, she couldn't see the future, but, when she met me, the pictures in her mind became clearer to her. I brought her to her climax: spiritually, mentally, and physically. She enjoyed my company. She told me her story, and I listened attentively. I relaxed her. She loved me, and, in return, I hurt her terribly.

What I did was wrong. I am man enough to admit it. But I never expected her to leave everything behind, including her family—even though her reasons were valid.

I will neither apologize nor justify my actions. Life is a lesson that should be learned from. I don't have any regrets. I loved her. I should have loved her more. I'm older and wiser; I know better now.

She constantly invades my mind. She never realized how much I loved her. She was a vitamin to my immune system; she meant a lot to me. I knew she loved me. I'd see it whenever I looked into her eyes, whenever she said a word to me, whenever we touched each other—everything we did together felt right.

> When she is next to me,
> time takes wing and speedily flies away.
> Without her, time stands still.
> The days between seeing her take an eternity.

I envy nothing from life but love. I will search the grounds on earth until I find it, and I will look into the skies, way above the firmaments and ask him to help me, and intervene if she is far away. I will plead my case and beg him to send me a chariot and have his eyes take me to her—or to let my hands beat the light air and fly like wings.

Distance is a measure that doesn't concern me. The anticipation of a reunion bolsters my spirit. William Shakespeare wrote in *Romeo in Juliet,* "Parting is such sweet sorrow." Everyone can understand the sorrows of parting ways. It is the sweetness of embracing her again that keeps my spirit aflame. The dark clouds must disappear, and the flames of light will once again burn.

> Look at the clouds; they're white and still.
> Love lies low with me through the night
> and arises like the sun with all its splendor.
> For so long, it was muted.
> Love, no longer whisper to me,
> but speak out loud.
> Love, life, and she are one to me.
> If I lose one, I lose not one but all three.

I love her like the morning loves dew. I knew who she was the very first day I laid my eyes on her. She is so special to me; she is my only in this fast world.

I sleep at night hoping she will visit me in my dreams, and she does, for when I wake up, I think of her, and I long for the day or night when we will meet again.

I owe her kisses and I owe her hugs. My lips haven't forgotten her, nor has my tongue forgotten the way she tastes. My being can still feel the heat of her body, and my chest can still feel the rhythmic vibration of her pulse and heart-beats—when we cuddled in bed. My love for her grows every single day.

Love is something my body needs and wants. My appetite for sex, and my hunger pains for love have left my stomach growling and my lips dry. Love is the remedy for my soul. It is the only thing that cleanses my body from the filthiness of this world.

Lord, let the fountains of her youth quench my thirst and let the heat of our bodies keep each other warm. Let my tongue lick her in many places when I find her, and let my lips always kiss her. Let twain become one. Let me love her forever. Let her understand my ways, and I hers. I want her underneath my arms once again to feel the heat of my body, my spirit, and the energy within my soul.

For that flame inside of me
slowly arises like the sun,
and increases its heat and glow as the day goes by,
and unlike how the sunset,
it doesn't fade away.

Love is a wide-open field.
The grass is greener with her,
and without her, it withers away.

When I was a teenager, my testosterone carried me for years. Today I no longer see a woman as a sexual object, but I see her as a soul and as a companion to converse with. Today I understand the paradox of love, the violence that unites couples in intimacy, and the securities that come when the soul feels comforted. You haven't lived if you haven't loved. My life is many stories, and it is a journey that has yet to be fulfilled.

Poems

I Understand It

My eyes were opened
and I saw,
my mind comprehended,
and I envisioned the future from afar.
I walked forward
to encounter,
the silence and numbness brought fear,
so I spoke.
I touched and felt,
I caressed and grabbed,
then learned and dealt with it.
Here is its name.

Yesterdays Were Wonderful Years

Yesterdays were wonderful years
to be innocent and young.
Inspiring were the promises of the future
and what is to come.
The matrimonies of it all,
enjoying and experiencing life.
Each day that passed by,
learned something new.

Hope's striving,
while dreams lead the way.
You refused to worry,
so reality was ignored
and sat down and waited,
knowing the odds were in his favor.

We all dream and look upon a star,
then say, "This will be one day."
Some dreamers escape their tribulations
with determination and hard work.
Some find God, and he shows them the way.
But the majority of dreamers who dream stop dreaming
because they were absorbed by the harsh realities of this world
now whisper out loud,
"Yesterdays were wonderful."

Shadow

The image of the nights,
the polite light in the dark,
spark up controversy by being a stalker.
It is just another adversity
and misfortune of his luck.
He is stuck being a follower,
while admiring the freedom of life.
The widow of the day
and the wife of the nocturnal
unleash unsolved mysteries of the internal soul.
He is the evil
and the obscure side of men.
I am his idol,
and he is the one
who does portray to be me,
my shadow.

The Shadow

(A Love Letter) A Love Song

Hear my love song and sensuous poem. This is from the entity that drives my soul—and to whom I seek attention from. I will not lie to you, being denied the freedom to express any type of emotions toward you because some people fear that I might confuse you.

And you will see this as something else, and not as poetry. Lit the fire within me, call passion, and intensify its flames.

They told me: Be politically correct. Write her a poem that is inspirational. Don't let your mind travel too much. Any sign of affection from you will be seen as a plea for romance.

It obvious I don't believe that. I disregarded everything they told me and defended my instinct. I know you will understand where I'm coming from. Intelligence is written all over your face.

On Valentine's Day you mentioned to me that my brother and I were your valentines. You know we love you. I wrote you this letter and poem to commemorate that day.

In my innocence
I will serenade you with poetry
and make love to you with words
and imagine things,
such as us cuddling and kissing,
as if you were my woman, my world
and talk about your silky hair
and your tender lips
and tell you thing for like.
How gently I could nibble on your nipples
and work my way down slowly to your hips.
Darling in my innocence,
I tell you these words.
This is from your boy, Joel.
My heart speaks to

Take Nothing for Granted

Soft loving and smooth kissing,
lots of hugging as she entered into uncharted territories
known as the abyss.

Tender times and precious moments,
love so sweet and well-defined,
my mind wandered off afar
and visualized a life with her—full of romances.

My heart was overwhelmed with feelings,
while my soul
begged my body for more.

It wanted her soft and plump lips,
her dreamy legs and thick hips,
her galvanizing smile and perfect face,
her curvaceous bosom and voluptuous body.

Even my spirit (tempted by flesh) pleaded to me,
to completely surrender to intimacy
and to allow us to take our fill of love every morning and evening.

Glorious days and phantom nights,
faith had me believing the unseen,
while dreary thoughts persecuted me with lustful dreams
that felt good, but weren't right.

With love so grand and hope pretending,
I succumbed to the everlasting flows and components of life,
and dove head first into the sea of love.

I wanted my dreams to submerge in water, be revitalized and
    reborn.
And as I swam to the center of the ocean looking for her,
my heartbeat stopped for three seconds,
I saw her drowning.

It took all my strength and every fiber of my soul to rescue her
and bring her back to shore.
When she opened her eyes, I knew my world was right before.

I've learned my lesson and that is to beware of nature,
and everything isn't always about me.
From now on I will solace her with love,
let us all solace ourselves with love.

Come Back Home

Come back home my love
and enter into the door of my heart.
I've sought pleasure from fools
and the joy that I comprehended not.
Render happiness,
that tender unexpected emotion, to my soul.
You delighted my spirit
and revealed to me a bright light
that outshines the sun.
Return to me
and let the debt I owe to you
be repaid.
My life without you,
just isn't the same.

My Love Affair With an Angel

(A Short Story)

Her hips and her lips
were soft and tender,
full of life, a new song.
Her wooly and curly hair
was so fair and beautiful.
She was a princess to many, but a queen to me.
Her brown eyes and caramel skin
were as glorious as the blue skies.
The way she presented herself was newsworthy.
She was an angel,
a delicate rose garden,
my beloved sweetheart, my shining star.
Her breasts were the pillows that comforted me.

When she rode the black stallion, her journey was always tumultuous and stormy. When I touched certain spots in her body, she hollered. I searched her cavity thoroughly (the fountains of her youth).

As we continued our journey, waters sprang forth abundantly in the midst of clouds. In the midst of her clouds, I'd enter into the gates of heaven and foreseen paradise, a peaceful world.

My eyes saw only love while my ears heard nothing but sweet melodies. My heart didn't only beat, but also sang. The sound of happiness vibrated throughout my soul.

Bewildered and amazed, I gazed at the environment and beheld the manifestation of ecstasy. Then suddenly, there appeared a light as bright as the sun coming toward me. The brightness of it blinded me. It was an angel, with wings, wearing a white gown.

She introduced herself to me. Her name was Leah. She said to me, "I'm your guardian angel. Your prayers have been heard. You are looking for love. Come closer to me and let me massage your chest."

The moment she touched me, my blood began to boil, and my veins felt like they were about to burst. I asked her what she was doing to me.

She replied, "Relax, I'm expanding your heart. I'm going to show you another dimension to this world you would have disregarded if I weren't here."

As she stared into my brown eyes, she said, "You must look beyond the depths of your vision. And seek out love from the beginning of your beloved nativity. Your voyages for love shall not be denied, but visited. She made herself known to you, and you flirted with her. Do you remember?"

For a brief second my heartbeat stopped, and for many days my mind traveled.

I replied, "Yes, she deeply impacted my life. She was the reason I've evolved as a person. I couldn't defend myself against her. She inspired me. I respected her a whole lot. She brought meaning to my life. I love and adore her."

I paused and reminisced:

Dreaming was my inspiration
when I first met her.
Very strong did I become
when she climbed the infinite ladder of my mind,
then entered through the doors of my heart.
She was the love of my life,
and the jewel that I treasured.
She was above all to me,
and I can't measure the unlimited joy
and all sorts of pleasure
that I've experienced today because of her.
I wanted us to spend our tomorrows together,
and shine as one light,

and one soul,

yesterday, now, and forever.

My mind sometimes envisioned life with her. For it knows life is a dream that is supposed to be mimicked. This world is an illusion. And when I fully understand that, it will become real.

Where is she? Leah responded, "Your spirit will guide you to her."
I asked her, "Is she far away?"
Leah did not respond. Her silence irritated me.
"How am I supposed to find her? She has blindfolded me in a crowded room."

Leah ripped off a piece of cloth from her gown and handed it to me. When I looked at it, I saw that it was a map with detailed directions.

I read the instructions, and they said, "Get out of the box, and find your way. Don't look back, follow the pathway. Keep walking until you reach your destination. There will be something there waiting for you. It will be a package; open it up. Rejoice, it is a gift."

Once I'd finished examining the map she gave me, Leah told me to look into her eyes. When I did, she told me to kiss her. The moment I kissed her, love consumed my heart. The heat that had my blood boiling simmered down. My body felt weightless.

Leah told me again, this time with a loud voice, "Your spirit will guide you to her." After she said that to me, she vanished into the thin air. She was right. My spirit led me to the destination where the map had instructed me to go. Once I'd arrived there. I saw a colorful box on top of a huge rock. I immediately opened up the package; the gift was a book.

I looked at it, turned the pages, and marveled at amazing pictures, which a phenomenal artist drew with words. That moment, I stopped skimming through the pages and put the book down. I began to glide and fly without propulsion, and I traveled through flashes of light, until I was brought back to my original condition and position, and once again was with her.

My flesh was rubbing against her flesh. My body was warm from the heat of our affections. The friction of our skin released a scent of musk in the air. Wanting more enjoyment and complete satisfaction, I continued to thrust and thrust until water sprang out from the midst of clouds.

She clung to me after we were done. We continued to cuddle and comfort each others' souls. She held my hands. Then, she leaned on me and kissed me.

> Her hips and her lips
> were soft and tender,
> full of life, a new song.

Once she kissed me, I remembered everything. Things I shouldn't have forgotten: those soft, precious lips, able to satisfy every inch and ounce of a body, and even rehabilitate souls. (Although the eyes are the windows to the soul, I've learned that a kiss can tell you everything.)

Still kissing, our tongues tied in a knot. My right hand caressed her buttocks while my fingers gently stroked her hair. I remember.

> Her wooly and curly hair
> was so fair and beautiful.
> She was a princess to many, but a queen to me.

And as I untied the knot of extreme bliss, I was still caught up in the moment, and galvanized by her sweet tastes. I leaned back to look at her, my mind wanting confirmation. I remember.

> Her brown eyes and caramel skin
> were as glorious as the blue skies.
> The way she presented herself was newsworthy.

I whispered to her, "Diane, Rachael, Leah." Once I said that her face changed to all the lovers I ever had. Leah was stunned that I had figured it out. She looked at me with lustful eyes, then said to me, "About time. I have a package I must give you."

Once she gave it to me, she vanished. (Little did I know.)

My beloved sweetheart was an angel,
a delicate rose garden,
a bright light, a shining star.
Her breasts were the pillows that comforted me.

Now she's gone. I unwrapped the gift she gave me. It was a book. This time I read it.

I cried when I realized what I had done. Lost in my own ways, I'd wandered to a place where corruption breeds. What I truly wanted and desired was heavenly, and not of this world.

For six days I lamented at home because of my thoughtless acts, and in the seventh day, my conscience also bearing me witness. I knelt down to pray to the Lord.

Lord, I humbly come before you with passion and love, desiring intimacy with her in its highest form. I can deliver to her the goods, and easily satisfy her body and mind with a gentle touch and smooth words. But my conscience troubles me, because I know better. I'm a mortal man, and my body is flesh.

When I was a child and my mind was able to comprehend existence, my thoughts, my passions, my love, my hope, my salvation, and all my dreams were with you.

Your ways are beyond us. You search the hearts of men. I wish I could run to heaven where the sun is bright, and stay, there I moonlight, all night long. But I can't. My love can only take me so far.

God of gods who rules, and watches existence majestically in his throne. Please forgive me, for my flesh is weak. I understand why you brought her into my life, and took her away from me.

Let the wings of love carry me to the promised land, and bring me one step closer to you. For love is where you are. Your loving is the truth.

Love Waits

Many lonely days
and many sleepless nights,
love without.
I still have no doubt
that I shall find love,
that gift from above,
whom I can call my own.

My afflictions and sacrifices,
fortify me with desire,
which provides me with strength.
Love will have mercy on me
and reward me with happiness
and extreme bliss.

Timeless King

Timeless King, please find me love.
Redeemer of Souls,
I beg you to bind up my wounds
and regenerate the opulence of love within my being
that only you can navigate.
Author of Life, for me,
make a decree to your subject.
Counselor of Humanity,
send the messenger
and announce her name to me.
For with hope, our hearts will gravitate toward the right path,
and, with faith, we will harmonize as one.
The Miracle Worker,
let her be the nurse that helps me.
And Everlasting Power,
the mortal flesh that takes care of me
while I perform my duties as a man.
Master of Ceremonies,
plan the festival
and hear me, Majesty, as I plead my case to you for my wife.
You are the Divine One who notarizes covenant.
And the only Judge with rulings
that are final and good.
Lord, she only do I want,
for my eyes shall not wander in search, desiring another.
She alone will suffice me with affection
and win over my heart and ears
with daily doses of conversations.
Our life together will be spent as one.

This is my deposition and oath to you,
for her—that virtuous women, my love, my wife.

(My Eyes See) Let Us Dance

Let us two dance as one in a bubble.
Let us float relentlessly in the firmament of the skies,
while we are being pedaled by the movement of our feet,
and our rhythm bounces us from wall to wall,
while our heartbeats pump defiantly.

Let our souls form an alliance for civility,
for our destination has no boundaries.
Join me.
Let twain and become one.
For I live only to mandate myself to you
and eternal love.

How Far Will I Go?

How far can I go?
And how far can my arms stretch
and my legs walk
to reach the top of the mountain?

How far can I see?
I looked up toward heaven and watched
birds fly together in formation
to their destination.

While I'm alone in this world,
and not by the laws of physics,
but in thought.

The white clouds move slowly though the blue skies.
And from all four corners of the earth,
the wind beats on me,
hitting my body with summer breezes.

I closed my eyes,
and with hope I visualized,
and with faith I surrendered too
and was carried away.

In my dreams, nothing I wanted was unattainable,
I reopened my eyes with answers to a new beginning.
I will not rest till I reach the peak of the mountain.

How far will I go?
Beyond where my eyes can see,
and my mind envision,

and as far as the wings underneath my soul

carry me.

How Long Will I?

How long will I let simplicity control my heart?
I have lost the fire and anger
that is required to overcome all sorts
of problems and dangers that I shall encounter.
I will abandon simplicity
and search out the power of knowledge.

How long will I allow myself to be bought?
I teach and preach lies for economic resource.
I have sold my soul to the devil,
for things that are worth naught.
I taught many things that weren't true,
and I expect to be respected,
for all the words that I knew,
that I had spoken to be false.
I will abandon the lies
and search out the power of knowledge.

How long will I continue to lie on my back
and let the stranger take advantage
and viciously attack me
whenever he pleases?
I wait for the assistances of others
and depend on the world for the bread that I need.
I will abandon the dependency I have on others
and search out the power of knowledge.

How long will I not take care of my child?
How long will I live my life reckless and wild?
How long will I continue to do things that aren't right?
How long will I represent darkness and not light?

I will abandon the how longs
and search out the power of knowledge.

I'm Hurting

Bad vibrations flow though the air. They echo sounds that mimic voices, which confound many who chose to hear. The lascivious and distorted words of those who lie about nothing and everything.

I'm hurting
and flirting with the thought of my nonexistence.
I am depressed,
and I'm stressed out to the limit.
I don't submit to the suns rays
that beam upon my eyes.
So why am I relying on and considering death?
I understood not the plots of life:
the necessity of adversity
and a man's will to stand
when he falls.
I'm blind,
but not lame.
And I am sick of,
but I will claim, love.
And the harsh pits of vanity
rule me not,
but the sanity of my humanity.

(A Love Letter) Pull My Strings

I've searched out all the vicinities of my soul
and patched up the holes,
for you and me
and us to be.
I love you as time does eternity,
and in my heart will you remain,
as long as I have life in me.
You have invaded my mind
and preoccupied my thoughts.
My wings of love
are flying high in heaven,
and the strings of my being
need your tender hands to pull and play.
The way you touch me,
there is nothing on earth that I can compare it to.
I savor every moment we share together
and retrieve them constantly from my memory.
Your hair is braided like a queen,
and when I look into your eyes,
the windows of your soul tell me everything.
Your lips are soft as silk,
and your skin is aloe to my flesh.
Your breasts, my hand enjoys
and your nipples, my mouth loves.
From the belly to your thighs I will not say,
but you know.
Your legs arouse me.
My darling,
I love you from head to toes.
I need your tender hands to pull my strings,

while I fly in heaven with wings of love
and make music.

(My Eyes See) I'm a Product

A talented man is a man with a cause,
a gifted soul,
shown us all and was.
A barrier withstood,
a survivor introduces,
an ultimate sacrifice
prolongs the agony,
but eventually produces
Life forces.
God will,
the glacier ice frosts,
the sun's heat prevails.
Energy circulates
and speed travels,
the voices echo vibration,
and the sounds unravel
and was heard.
To do is to be,
and what is new
is fuel for today,
and tomorrow an old idea.
I think and dream
and became what existence is?
His,
the Author of life product.

Fallen Angel

Fallen angel, underneath the sun,
Fallen angel, what have you done?

Fallen angel, you made me cry.
Fallen angel, please tell me why?

You were everything to me,
possibly the love of my life.

All day did our souls blush
as we danced with each other.

Fallen angel, you were wrong.
Fallen angel, now you're gone.

(A Love Letter) There Are Angels on Earth

How is it
that my heart envies what I feel for you?
And how is it
that my mind envisions an angel,
and there you were standing right in front of me,
and I had not a clue?
Understanding is the beginning of knowledge,
and to discover and create a plot
shows the maturity of him that diligently wanted to learn.
So, yes, I do know now
that my eyes were blessed from seeing you,
and I will confess
that I hadn't seen a stunning women until I'd met you.
As divine as you are,
I can only worship one God,
and while I wish that we could be,
my mind and body and soul already belong to another.
So what can a man do?
Who acknowledges that in this world
there are few who possess true beauty
that I love and also admire?
The question has been answered.

I Stand

The bastard attacked me with a sword in his hand.
He'd chained me up with iron
then brought me to this land.
For centuries I worked for free,
and like cows I was branded—
I'm stranded in his world,
while freedom searches for me—
Independence Day arrived
and the bastard declared to me liberty.
He promised me forty acres and a mule,
and fueled me with laws and utterances
that I have yet to see.
Dreams occurred and now I may vote,
and dreams succored me
and brought me false hope.
New jails are being built
while old schools are refurbished
I'm presumed guilty
until proven innocent,
and I am tried in the fire of his furnace.
I ask myself,
Who is damned, me or this man?
I journey the quests of resistance and torture,
without food or land to call my own,
and still
I stand.

Isn't She?

Her image is spiritual
and her beauty infinite.
Her thoughts are ravishing
and her ideas astute.
Her glory is everlasting
and her face shines.
Her presence is felt
and her reach high.
Her streak continues
and her mission accomplished.
Her strength is overwhelming
and her loyalty toward God.
I am in love with her,
for she is the royalty
that crowns kings.

(My Eyes See) To the One I Love

Oh to the one that I love,
I bow down the knees of my heart.
You, lover of souls,
such precious stones
as diamonds and gold
mean nothing to me.
You never belied me
continue to dally and play with me.
And let not my eyes wander in search for you,
for I am not lost.
Priceless is my life,
but for you
I die for no cost.
You are the first Author of Beauty.

Splash the Water with Waves

Splash the water with waves.
The evildoer of the earth
continues to corrupt the world and misbehave.
Revolt and you shall be saved.
The just will overcome the wicked
and bring their tormentors to their graves.
The rich abhor the poor,
leaving them with crumbs that remain in the table
and not a penny more.
The earth is broken up and shattered.
The peoples are scattered abroad and do not matter.
They persist to cut down the trees with their axes,
and continue to suck men dry with their taxes.
Cry out for a leader
and let the savior arise.
Our lives—and their demise—depend on it.

(My Eyes See) The Earth Remains

The eclipse shines
and the sun sparks.
The sea roars,
while Sons of men balk.
The tree stands
and the eagle lands.
The fish swim,
while the plans of Sons of men
damn the earth.
The water splashes
and the fire burns.
The past becomes history,
while Sons of men return
as exhibits in museums.
God, look at,
then take back,
and then put peace and order in this world.

(A Love Letter) Let Me Sing

I've been through lot of things, and that one day and night of hell we dealt with together has changed my whole concept of life and how I feel about you. Everything has a season and a time, such as the eclipse of the moon, the bears when they hibernate, and the weather with its tremendous forces. And mine finally—did, and it was long overdue. And because of it, I am singing to you the blues.

> I can never stay mad at you,
> I just can't.
> Nor will I ever hate you,
> for my heart won't allow it.
> And as the rose pedals blossom into their voluptuous forms,
> and the scent arouses bees,
> that odor and beauty
> will I only allow myself to smell and see from you.
> Love is too much of a powerful emotion,
> for me to confuse it and not use it.
> The Master Technician has fixed my organ,
> and he has pumped up the volume,
> and played the music.
> Hear my melodies and lyrics,
> and whenever the stage or podium doesn't frighten you,
> get up and sing the song.
> My heart sings a cappella.

Who Is the Man?

Who can conquer the conqueror?
Or dwells with the possessor of the earth?
Who can outshine the sun?
Or even transform air into dirt?
I can flirt with a woman.
But who can with destiny?
I can outlast numerous decades.
But who preserves time?

Either–Or

Roll down your windows
and follow the breezes.
Go where the wind goes
escape the debris.

Or

Labor for the wind,
and pretend the days of your life aren't numbered.
From beginning to end,
dusk till dawn,
morning and night,
daylight, sunset,
vanity, vexation of spirit,
understand there is nothing that profits underneath the sun.

(Genesis chapter 2:7 He breathed into his nostrils the breath of life, and man became a living soul.) The stories of our lives, the brilliances of his excellency, before we were put into his inventory, freed our minds and gave us choices. Just to establish?

Time flies
while the wind passes you by.

Roll down your windows
and follow the breezes.
Go where the wind goes
escape the debris.

Or.

(My Eyes See) Have Mercy

I seek repentance for all the deeds that I have done wrong.
And I bow down to mercy, for pretending I was strong.
Am I not a manly god, and do I not have an everlasting spirit,
And a king that existence nodded repeatedly to?
Who am I to blend love with sin?
And what being have I created to beguile my soul from within?
Can I pose better than a still picture?
And can I expose a secret, which wasn't meant for men,
that was sealed by a God?
Let my eyes weep for joy
and my soul live to thirst and feed,
for the leniency of the Deliverer.

Preview of the novel *The Forbidden Fruit* written in parables and metaphors.

My mind could never imagine, nor could I ever envision the days and nights I was tempted by the flesh—and how all my emotions betrayed me, and at the end of the day, left me stranded and alone. My heart was heavy with lust and my soul was pondering its ways, begging for tomorrow. Just to collect my mind, I'd wander in the woods, where the birds cry every morning, and the wolves howl in the evening, and the bears stalk their prey at night.

For endless love, I walked though the jungles of Brooklyn, New York, with a righteous heart. My vision was blinded; there were so many distractions. My ears heard echoes—it was sound in it vibrating form. People were muttering and grumbling under their breaths. They were whispering to each other, saying, "He is going to break her heart again."

They had no idea that I could hear them. I laughed in my heart while I listened to their rhetoric and walked away from them.

My body was extremely fatigued, but my mind remained focused. I visualized her, and the mere thought of seeing her again kept me going. I couldn't escape her, nor could I hide my feelings for her any longer. She was all I wanted and all I needed.

Paradise is no longer on earth, but the forest still has lots of trees, and the fields harvest lots of fruit. As I journeyed though the vineyards and plantations and tarried at certain branches for days, my conscious troubled me. I was awed by the loveliness and beauty of each limb, and I was fascinated by the colors and decorations and by how diverse the branches were.

To my amazement, there wasn't a single thorn—just seeds scattered everywhere. I picked up a few grains along the way and planted them toward the sun. I also nourished them with water. Spring arrived, and many flowers blossomed and grew. But there was one that stood out—with qualities and features that were clearly distinguishable from the rest.

She was edible and ready to be ripe. My lips wanted to taste her; my tongue wanted to nibble; and my teeth very gently bite. She had bloomed into perfection—even her latitude on earth needed no correction.

I had every intention to claim her and reap the benefits for tilling the ground, but her voluptuous form and agreeable scent aroused bees. She truly was a sight to be seen, and a peril worthy to visited. She was a mirage that was real and natural, just like a waterfall at the end of a river.

I'd marvel every time I looked at her. Her beauty overwhelmed me. I'd never felt this way before in my life. Out of pure lust for her, I scrutinized everything that she did. Just inhaling what I'd seen dumbfounded me; that fine specimen from an organic world overshadowed every species around her.

> My eyes have witnessed beauty,
> which causes my soul to blush,
> now my spirit urges for her,
> while my flesh yearns to touch.

She had stimulated my mind and hardened my bones. She was so surreal; I felt like I was in another dimension better known as heaven, openly receiving a token from God that I surely didn't deserve. To me, she was a symbol of his grace and the excellence of his best.

I lifted up my head and hands toward heaven and saluted the skies for bringing forth a misgiving coming. The rainbow was covering her. It only magnified her beauty even more from the things surrounding her.

She was like a rose with pedals full of life. She was the spark of the day and the impetus light at night. She was glorious, and I wanted her in every way. She was as the evergreen, her momentum increased with time.

How beautiful?
How sweet?
She is so pleasant to the eyes,
even my lids and pupils weep
and cry for her.
I am a man
who only wants what he needs,
but now desire has occupied my thoughts,
while lust devours my heart
for instant gratification.

(Skipped to page 12)

(Kiwi blindfolded me and whispered into my right ear).

"Trust me. I will not let anything happen to you."

She held my hand as we walked for miles. I didn't question her once.

Water was flowing though the rocks. The scent of roses was in the air. Lilies were everywhere. She had brought me to a brook, a small river that was inside a cave. It wasn't visible from the outside. She had to lead me in.

As I followed her inside, I heard the voices of kids. They were swimming in the river. I took off my shirt and pants and dove right in. The water was warm. Some of the kids rushed toward me and asked me to play with them, and I did for a few hours.

When I got out of the river, she brought me a towel and a robe. I used the towel to dry myself off. When I was finished, I covered my waist with it. I put on the robe and took off my briefs, which were wet. She was resting on a comforter, waiting patiently for me. She tapped the ground and said, "When you're done, come here."

I was exhausted. I lay down next to her and closed my eyes and fell asleep. She woke me up three hours later when all the kids finally got out of the river and went home. Ten minutes after they left, she jumped into the river and asked me, "Joel, join me."

I kindly rejected her offer and told her, "Have fun."

Kiwi laughed, got out of the river, and sat right next to me. She began to kiss me on the left side of my neck and started to bite my chest. She stopped for a second, looked directly into my eyes, and attempted to kiss me on my lips. I nodded my head. She said, "I want to taste you."

I replied, "I have rules."

With her left hand, she grabbed my penis and yanked it, and as she pulled, she looked at me with a smirk in her face.

"I want you inside of me," she said.

I replied, "We can play the game as long as you follow the rules. The rules are: do not kiss me on the lips because you will remind me of her, and stop biting me while you are kissing me. Are you purposely trying to put scars on my flesh?"

Kiwi answered, "All right, let's continue. I will stop biting you, and I will follow your rules." (Twenty seconds later she grabbed my face and attempted to kiss me on my lips again.)

"What are you doing?" I asked her.

Kiwi replied, "I couldn't help myself."

I told her, "These are simple rules. The reason I'm here with you is because I'm trying to get Diane out of my mind. Get off me. Today I realized I cannot shift my heart from one person to another."

At that moment, she jumped on me and began to wrestle with me. She tore the robe off me and snatched the towel from my waist. I was naked. She ran to the brook and threw all the articles of clothing that I had into the river.

She smiled. Then she charged toward me, as if she were a bull, and wrestled with me again. She pushed and pulled me and slapped and pounded my chest with her hands. She scratched my back with her fingernails. She was kicking my ass. I didn't resist.

Only after she aggressively went after my genitals did I lift her up off her feet and put her on my shoulders. I ran toward the brook and jumped into the river with her—then I splashed water at her.

I asked her, "Do you still want to play the game?"

"Yes I do," she replied.

She took off her blouse and skirt and started to kiss me again. Wow, she was hot. I never realized how lovely she was. She was always covered up. Her body was a work of art. It captivated me. It was flawless from head to toe. I was aroused.

My tongue and lips played with the bottom of her ears, while my teeth bit them gently. She kissed and bit the top of my chest. She wasn't following the rules, but I continued to play with her. I pushed her hair aside and started to kiss both sides of her neck. I took my time; I wasn't in a rush.

Next I kissed her shoulders, while my hands caressed her breasts. With my middle and index fingers, I pulled her nipples, and, as my hands moved in a circular motion, I let them go. As time passed by, I began to explore her breasts with my mouth. My tongue played with her nipples; with my teeth, I gently nibbled on them, pulled, and let go. She quivered.

"No one has ever done that to me before. I love it," she told me.

"You're still young," I replied.

She smiled, "Do it again. I want you to touch my pussy and see how wet it is."

I did. With my left hand, I squeezed her bosom, and my right hand brushed firmly against her belly as it reached for her vagina. It was extremely wet. I massaged it with my fingers for a while. She grabbed my penis and yelled at me, "Put it in."

My penis was harder then a roll of coins. I wanted her as badly as she wanted me. Our private parts kept touching. She was massaging her vagina with my penis. I moved a few steps backward to collect my thoughts. I grabbed and held her hands, then looked directly into her eyes and said with a low voice, "Do you want me?"

"Yes," she said.

I grabbed the back of her neck and brought her closer to me. I tasted the air as she spoke to me. I didn't kiss her, even though I wanted to. I asked her again, "Do you want me?"

"Yes," she said.

"You know my heart is with Diane," I told her.

Kiwi replied, "I know."

"So you know I must leave now and get out of this river," I responded.

She looked at me with a disgruntled face and didn't say a word. I got out of the river and whispered to her, "Good-bye."

(Skipped to last page in Chapter 1)

My heart has been led astray. Diane has paralyzed my thoughts and has taken my emotions into captivity. I was slowly gravitating toward her. I could feel her oral, her presence was endearing.

I knew she wasn't far away; I ran through the forest as fast as I could until I saw her. When I did, I stopped and yelled out, "Diane, Diane, Diane."

When she heard me calling out her name, she stopped walking and began to look for me. Then she saw me.

My body trembled as I got closer to her. It took me five minutes to get to her. Then I was next to her. She stared into my eyes and began to blush. I grabbed her hand and held it firmly.

Tears were falling from my eyes. I'd waited for this day; I had longed for this day. Six years had felt like a lifetime. Then she was crying. I hugged her, and for ten minutes, we cried together. I never uttered a word to her; my tears spoke for me. I finally did and said.

Chapter 2—The Courtship Begins

Diane asked, "Joel why did you leave me?"

I told her, "Love's course is never a straight road."

But she insisted, "I really want to know. Tell me why."

I replied, "Today is the beginning of a new day. Please allow us to enjoy it, and let me plead my case to you tomorrow. Let us take our fill of love until the morning. Today, let us solace ourselves with love."

My Eyes See
Volume Two

Written by
Joel Sejour

My world has darkened in the midst of darkness
while the light in my eyes has dimmed.
Fortunately for me,
the light that guides me
never abided in my eyes,
but stays and tarries in my soul.
I can see the light at the end of the tunnel.
And I will shine with it,
undoubtedly here, and wherever I go,
in this dark place, this dark world.

This Isn't My World
(An excerpt)

This isn't my world,
where the land is filled with fools,
where people are void of understanding,
and the nations doomed.

This isn't my world,
where lies and darkness rule.

My Eyes See

Volume 2

and

The Forbidden Fruit

will be available

later this year.

The song title

"My Eyes See"

is written by

Samson and Sejour.

Notes

For comments and questions, you can contact us by e-mail at,
joelsejour@yahoo.com,
or at www.myspace.com/samsonandsejour

978-0-595-34807-7
0-595-34807-6

Printed in the United States
204929BV00001B/409-423/P